JANE AUSTEN

JANE AUSTEN

A. Susan Williams

Life and Works

Jane Austen
The Brontës
Thomas Hardy
Hemingway
D. H. Lawrence
Katherine Mansfield
George Orwell
Shakespeare
H. G. Wells
Virginia Woolf

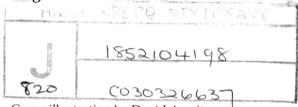
Cover illustration by David Armitage

First published in 1989 by
Wayland (Publishers) Ltd
61 Western Road, Hove
East Sussex BN3 1JD, England

Series adviser: Dr Cornelia Cook
Series designer: David Armitage
Editor: Sophie Davies

British Library Cataloguing in Publication Data

Williams, A. Susan
  Jane Austen – (Life and works).
  I. Title   III. Series
  823'.7

  ISBN 1–85210–419–8

Typeset by Kalligraphics Ltd, Horley, Surrey
Printed in Italy by G. Canale & C.S.p.A., Turin
Bound in the UK by Mac Lehose & Partners, Portsmouth

Contents

1 Jane Austen: Girl and Woman

The Austen family

'English verdure . . . seen under a sun bright' was for Jane Austen 'a sweet view – sweet to the eye and the mind.' She loved the countryside in which she spent most of her life. Her first 25 years were spent in the Hampshire village of Steventon, where she was born on 16 December 1775. Her father, the Reverend George Austen, was the rector of Steventon and the neighbouring parish of Deane. He and his wife Cassandra lived in Steventon Rectory with their growing family.

It has often been said that Jane was the sixth of seven children. But in fact, she was the seventh of eight: the second son was mentally handicapped and was cared for by another family in the neighbourhood. The existence of this boy is concealed in the *Memoir* of Austen's life that was written by her nephew. It is possible that the family felt ashamed of his disability.

Jane enjoyed being part of a large family. 'Children of the same family, the same blood, with the same first associations and habits', she observes in *Mansfield Park*, 'have some means of enjoyment in their power, which no subsequent connection can supply.' But the 'single most important person in Jane's life', said Mrs Austen, was her sister Cassandra. 'If Cassandra were to have her head cut off', she remarked, 'then Jane would have

hers cut off, too!' Jane never had a bedroom of her own but shared a room with Cassandra until her death. We can see a reflection of their close attachment in the several pairs of loving sisters in Austen's novels. Jane and Elizabeth in *Pride and Prejudice,* and Elinor and Marianne in *Sense and Sensibility,* show a similar devotion to each other.

A silhouette of Cassandra, Jane's sister and constant companion.

Opposite *Like Fanny in* Mansfield Park, *Jane's brother Edward was adopted by a rich family, the Knights.*

Jane was also fond of her brothers. The eldest, James, 'recommended the books which charmed her leisure hours, he encouraged her taste, and corrected her judgement', just as Edmund does for his cousin Fanny, in *Mansfield Park.* Jane's third brother, Edward, was adopted by some rich, childless relations called the Knights. He eventually took their name and inherited their large estates. The fourth brother, Henry, was Jane's favourite, and he became her faithful adviser in literary and practical matters.

9

Admiral Sir Francis Austen, one of Jane's two naval brothers. They both took part in sea battles against the French during the Napoleonic Wars (1799–1815).

The last two brothers, Francis and Charles, joined the navy at the age of 12, both rising to the rank of Admiral. Like Fanny's brother William in *Mansfield Park*, each of them 'had seen a great deal [and] had been in the Mediterranean – in the West Indies – in the Mediterranean again . . .[and] had known every variety of danger, which sea and war together could offer.' Jane took an active interest in the careers of Frank and Charles and evidently admired the navy. There are four naval officers

Commander Charles Austen, whose travels with the navy provided the West Indian background for Mansfield Park.

in *Persuasion*, all of whom are good men . . . and much more likeable than many of the other characters!

The social class to which the Austens belonged was the 'gentry'. The gentry lived off inherited wealth, but were not as rich as the aristocracy. Their social status was beneath the aristocracy but above the middle (professional and merchant) classes. Like many members of the gentry, however, the Austens had connections with the nobility, and there were still an abbey and a barony in the family. Jane's portrayal of this class in her fiction is therefore based on first-hand experience.

It is difficult for Austen's readers in the late twentieth century to discover and to understand the customs of the different classes at this time. Some of these customs, which were then accepted without question, may seem

to us rather odd. We might even be appalled to learn that Mrs Austen did not take care of her children when they were infants, but farmed them out to other families in the village. Jane's nephew tells us that:

> Her mother followed a custom, not unusual in those days, though it seems strange to us, of putting out her babies to be nursed in a cottage in the village. The infant was daily visited by one or both of its parents, and frequently brought to them at the parsonage, but the cottage was its home, and must have remained so till it was old enough to run about and talk.

Opposite *Admiral Croft in* Persuasion *is 'quite the gentleman in all his notions and behaviour'.*

Feeding up the wet nurse ensured the survival of the babies she was paid to breast-feed.

Steventon Rectory, Jane's home until she was twenty-five.

Life at Steventon

Jane's formal education was brief. At the age of 7, she went with Cassandra to a school in Southampton, but after a year they were brought home with a 'putrid fever'. Once they had recovered, they went to another school in Reading in Berkshire, where they stayed for a year and a half.

At the age of 11, Jane settled at home in Steventon. Although she no longer went to school, her education

was not neglected. She was taught classics by her father, learned French and some Italian, had lessons in playing the piano, and was taught domestic duties by her mother. The childhood of the Austen sisters was rather like that of the Bennet girls in *Pride and Prejudice:* 'such of us as wished to learn', declares Elizabeth, 'never wanted the means. We were always encouraged to read, and had all the masters that were necessary.' Jane read very widely, and she began to write fiction at the age of ten.

The Austen girls went to Church and performed parish duties, which included visits to the local poor. They were also busy with their 'work': their sewing, embroidery and netting. Girls of this class were proficient in all sorts of needlework. The young Mr Bingley

The Revd George Austen, Jane's father, took a keen interest in her writing.

in *Pride and Prejudice* observes that, 'They all paint tables, cover screens, and net purses. I scarcely know any one who cannot do all this, and I am sure I never heard a young lady spoken of for the first time without being informed that she was very accomplished'.

The whole family enjoyed acting. Between 1784 and 1790, they produced plays in the barn or the dining room, depending on the season. Perhaps Jane was recalling her own childhood when she wrote in *Mansfield Park* that: 'a love of the theatre is so general, an itch for acting so strong among young people'.

Edmund Bertram and Mary Crawford in the BBC production of Mansfield Park.

The move to Bath

In 1801, the Reverend Austen retired from his position as rector and took his wife and two daughters to Bath. This city, which has been famous since Roman times for its springs, which were supposed to be good for the health, had become a fashionable resort in the eighteenth century. By the time the Austens arrived, the glitter and gaiety were moving to Brighton. But it was still an attractive place to spend the 'season': it offered balls and concerts, as well as the chance of 'taking the cure'. When Mr Allen in *Northanger Abbey* is 'ordered to Bath for the benefit of a gouty constitution', his wife fills Catherine with 'eager delight' by asking her to join them.

But for Jane Austen, who was now 25, this was not a happy move. Like Anne Elliott in *Persuasion*, who is also forced to leave the countryside for a stay in Bath, she 'persisted in a very determined . . . disinclination for Bath'. Perhaps she also shared Anne's wonder that her father 'should find so much to be vain of in the littlenesses of a town.'

Bath was a popular resort in the eighteenth century but Jane Austen did not like it, and was unhappy when her family moved there in 1801.

Chawton Cottage, where Jane spent the last years of her life.

Chawton Cottage – Jane's last years

Only four years after the move to Bath, Jane's father died. The three Austen women then moved into lodgings. In the next year, 1806, they went to Southampton. Jane left Bath with 'happy feelings of escape' and certainly preferred the Hampshire city of Southampton. But she still longed to return to the country.

Jane preferred Southampton to Bath, but still missed the countryside.

At last, in 1809, she had her wish. Edward Knight, the brother who had been adopted by a rich family (whose name he had taken) and now had two large estates at his disposal, arranged for his mother and sisters to live in Chawton Cottage. The Hampshire village of Chawton was dominated by the Chawton Manor House, where Edward and his family lived when they were not on their Godmersham estate. Jane's pleasure at being back in the countryside must have been at least a little marred by the discomfort of being a poor relation to the wealthy Knights. The Austens could not even take part in social activities, since they could not afford a carriage and had to rely on a donkey and cart. One could hardly arrive at a county ball in a donkey cart! Not surprisingly, Jane wrote with sympathy about the difficulties of being a poor relation in *Mansfield Park*,

Edward Knight, Jane's brother, who arranged for his mother and sisters to live in Chawton Cottage on one of the estates he inherited from his adoptive parents.

A carriage was too expensive for the Austen women, so they rarely attended social functions.

one of the three novels written at Chawton.

Jane Austen was not blessed with a long life. After only seven years at Chawton, she developed a 'lingering illness' that caused fever and weakness. This illness is now thought to have been Addison's disease, a hormonal disorder. But it had not been identified by Austen's time and nothing could be done to prevent a rapid deterioration in her health. In the following year, at the age of 41, Jane went to Winchester with Cassandra to seek expert medical advice. There she died on 18 July 1817, in her sister's arms.

Love and romance

Some readers of Jane Austen's fiction assume that she showed little interest in men. This idea may have developed because she never married and because she and Cassandra 'were thought to have taken to the garb of middle age [wearing a cap and thus accepting spinsterhood] unnecessarily soon.' But this comment by Jane's niece ignores the shortage of money that probably explained this style in dress.

Jane's family were reticent about her personal life, giving the impression that she was quite prim and proper. But her letters and other material reveal that she was as interested in love and romance as most people.

It does seem that she was a fairly awkward and shy adolescent and she was described at the age of 12 as 'not at all pretty and very prim'. Like Catherine Morland in *Northanger Abbey*, however, she matured into a confident young woman. Indeed, Jane and Cassandra were described in their late teens as 'perfect beauties and of course gain "hearts by the dozen".'

The house in Winchester where Jane died in her sister's arms.

In her twentieth year, Jane had her first important romance . . . and disappointment. She and a young man called Tom Lefroy became fond of each other and apparently made quite an exhibition of themselves in the neighbourhood. But neither Jane nor Tom had any money, and their families decided to separate them. 'The day is come on which I am to flirt my last with Tom Lefroy', wrote Jane to Cassandra, adding that 'when you receive this it will be over. My tears flow as I write at the melancholy idea'.

The heroine of *Persuasion* is similarly advised against marriage to a man without 'expectations'. But this fictional romance has a happy ending. Years later, the heroine meets her beloved again. He has now made his

Opposite Women's clothes in Austen's time were high-waisted and flowing. Young women, like Jane and her sister, who were expected to attract a husband, would have dressed like this.

Tom Lefroy, Jane's first love.

25

name and fortune in the navy and, after a series of
complications, they eventually decide to marry. It is possible to regard *Persuasion* as an attempt by Austen to
rewrite her own past. If so, we may conclude that Tom
did not reciprocate the depth of her attachment. For in
Persuasion, the love of a woman is shown to be more
enduring than that of a man.

In 1798, Jane attracted, but was not attracted by, a Mr Blackall. Then, four years later, while staying at the seaside, she became acquainted with a gentleman, 'whose charm of person, mind, and manners was such that Cassandra thought him worthy to possess and likely to win her sister's love.' Jane's nephew tells us that:

When they parted, he expressed his intention of soon seeing them again; and Cassandra felt no doubt as to his motives. But they never again met. Within a short time they heard of his sudden death. I believe that, if Jane ever loved, it was this unnamed gentleman; but the acquaintance had been short, and I am unable to say whether her feelings were of such a nature as to affect her happiness.

Manydown House, the home of the Bigg Withers. Jane would have lived here if she had not broken off her engagement to Harris Bigg Wither.

The marriages of Elinor and Marianne end a series of difficulties in Sense of Sensibility. *Here Edward Ferrars proposes to Elinor.*

In the same year, Jane accepted a proposal of marriage from a 21-year-old heir to a fortune called Harris Bigg Wither. But she withdrew her acceptance next morning! Her family were disappointed, and perhaps Jane recalled their dissatisfaction when she wrote in *Mansfield Park* of the Bertrams' irritation with Fanny at her refusal of Henry Crawford. Is it significant that Henry is shown to be a cad and a bounder? In any case, it seems that Jane, like Fanny, felt that 'a man [need not] be acceptable to every woman he may happen to like himself.'

When Jane was 32, she declined an offer of marriage from a clergyman four years younger than herself. In the autumn of the same year, he tried his luck with Cassandra . . . and was refused by her, too!

Engraving of Jane Austen in her nephew's Memoir *of her life. It makes her look prettier than the sketch (see page 7) from which it was taken.*

Evidently, Jane herself experienced the feelings of love and disappointment that inform her novels. But her vision of marriage was a realistic one. Like Elinor in *Sense and Sensibility*, she seems to have felt that in spite of 'all that is bewitching in the idea of a single and constant attachment, and all that can be said of one's happiness depending entirely on any particular person, it is not meant – it is not fit – it is not possible that it should be so.' Some readers may consider Jane's presentation of marriage as more cynical than realistic. Her novels seethe with unhappy marriages that are marred, to use Elinor's words, by 'the strange unsuitableness which often existed between husband and wife'.

Jane Austen's personality

James Austen-Leigh's *Memoir* of his aunt Jane Austen, which was published in 1870, established many impressions of her that are still prevalent today. It concludes the account of her death with the statement that:

> She was a humble, believing Christian. Her life had been passed in the performance of home duties, and the cultivation of domestic affections, without any self-seeking or craving after applause. She had always sought, as it were by instinct, to promote the happiness of all who came within her influence, and doubtless she had her reward in the peace of mind which was granted her in her last days. Her sweetness of temper never failed.

Such comments have helped to create a picture of Jane Austen as *terribly* good and *terribly* nice. It seems, however, that this was not quite the case and that she was by no means blessed with an unfailing 'sweetness of temper'. Indeed, a recent biographer has referred to her 'obvious moodiness, her occasional bad temper, her inclination towards sarcasm, cynicism and harsh judgement of others'. Certainly her letters reveal a biting sense of humour. In one letter to her sister, she wrote that 'Mrs Hall, of Sherborne, was brought to bed yesterday of a dead child, some weeks before she expected, owing to a fright. I suppose she happened to look unawares at her husband!' When her niece was staying in her bed at Chawton, she wrote home with the comment that 'I hope that she [finds] my Bed comfortable . . . and has not filled it with fleas'.

Many critics have looked for Jane Austen in her fictional heroines. But they are all such different women. Perhaps it would be wiser to assume that there is at least a little bit of Jane in each of them.

The position of women

The reader of *Emma* is likely to feel disappointed in Jane Fairfax's decision to marry Frank Churchill, who is inferior to her in every respect but wealth and rank. In *Pride and Prejudice*, Mrs Bennet's efforts to marry off her five daughters have an air of desperation. So, too, does Charlotte's decision to marry the contemptible Mr Collins, whose society 'was irksome, and his attachment to her must be imaginary.'

However, since women of the time were often forced to depend on men for their survival, the behaviour of these women is by no means inappropriate. Despite Jane's cleverness and beauty, she *needs* to marry Frank. Her only alternative is to become a governess, which she equates with slavery. While Mrs Bennet's obsession with marrying her daughters often leads to foolish and irritating behaviour, it is based on the hard fact of an entail – a legal document in this case stipulating that the heir to Longbourn must be male. It is hardly surprising that 'she continued to rail bitterly against the cruelty of settling an estate away from a family of five daughters, in favour of a man whom nobody cared anything about.' Charlotte's position is equally difficult. 'Without thinking highly either of men or of matrimony', explains Austen, 'marriage had always been her [Charlotte's] object; it was the only honourable provision for well-educated young women of small fortune, and however uncertain of giving happiness, must be their pleasantest preservative from want.'

Fay Weldon, the twentieth-century novelist and critic, explains that:

The trouble was that you had to be able to *afford* to marry. You were expected to have a dowry, provided by your parents or saved by yourself, to give to your husband to offset your keep. For this great reason, and a variety of others, only thirty per cent of women married. Seventy per cent remained unmarried. It was no use waiting for your parents to die so that you could inherit their mansion, or cottage, or hovel, and so buy yourself a husband – your parents' property went to your brothers. Women inherited only through their husbands, and only thus could gain access to property. Women were born poor, and stayed poor, and lived well only by their husbands' favour.

Opposite *Jane Fairfax in* Emma *is horrified at the prospect of being sold to the 'governess-trade' (this scene comes from the BBC production).*

'At the age of twenty-seven, without having ever been handsome, [Charlotte] felt all the good luck' of her marriage to the foolish Mr. Collins. (BBC production of Pride and Prejudice*)*

Opposite *Emma's wealth and status enlarge her freedom and she finds 'perfect happiness' with Mr. Knightley.*

Even rich women had a poor deal in comparison with men. When Maria Bertram in *Mansfield Park* has an adulterous affair after her marriage, she suffers social disgrace and is banished by her father to a cottage in the country. But no such punishment is imposed on her lover. 'That punishment, the public punishment of disgrace, should in a just measure attend *his* share of the

offence is, we know', comments Austen, 'not one of the barriers, which society gives to virtue. In this world, the penalty is less equal than could be wished.' Mary Bennet in *Pride and Prejudice* justly warns that 'loss of virtue in a female is irretrievable . . . one false step involves her in endless ruin . . . her reputation is no less brittle than it is beautiful.'

Maria Bertram, who is punished for adultery in Mansfield Park *(BBC).*

War and peace

A superficial reading of Austen's fiction may suggest that the England of her time was boring. But this was by no means the case. For one thing, it was a country at war. From the late 1700s until the Battle of Waterloo in 1815, two years before Jane's death, England was at war with France. Jane, like most well-educated people,

Napoleon at the Battle of Waterloo, 1815, where he was defeated by the British and the Prussians.

would have read about the war in the newspapers (*The Times* was established in 1788). Her naval brothers were another valuable source of information, since they took part in the battles at sea.

Opposite *The Battle of Trafalgar, one of the naval battles in the war against the French.*

The war with France followed the French Revolution, which began with the storming of the Bastille prison in Paris, in 1789. Jane's family was personally affected by the social upheaval on the other side of the English Channel. Her cousin Eliza had been educated in Paris and married a Count de Feuillide, who was guillotined in 1794. Jane's nephew tells us that:

> . . . he perished by the guillotine during the French Revolution . . . His wife escaped through dangers and difficulties to England, was received for some time into her uncle's [that is, Jane's] family, and finally married her cousin Henry Austen. During the short peace of Amiens, she and her second husband went to France, in the hope of recovering some of the Count's property, and there narrowly escaped being included amongst the *détenus*. Orders had been given by Buonaparte's government to detain all English travellers, but at the post-houses Mrs Henry Austen gave the necessary orders herself, and her French was so perfect that she passed everywhere for a native, and her husband escaped under this protection.

The state of the nation – poverty and class

The population of the British Isles in 1800 was 11 million, more or less (today it is well over 50 million). Most of these people were poor, and a few of them were rich. Poverty was even more terrible then than it is today, since there was no welfare state to act as a buffer against starvation and death. In *Letters to Alice*, Fay Weldon asks her fictional niece 'to conceive of England, your country, two hundred years ago.' She explains that it was:

> . . . a place without detergents or tissues or tarmaced roads or railway trains, or piped water, let alone electricity or gas or oil; where energy (what a modern term) was provided by coal, and wood, and the muscle of human beings, and that was all . . . [People] were so poor – most people – they would run, and toil, and sweat all day and all night to save themselves and their

Presenté par le Sr. cholats l'un des Vainqueur de la Bastil.

The storming of the Bastille in Paris, 1789, which marked the start of the French Revolution.

Siege de la Bastille Representé Au Naturel Le 14 Juillet 1789

Jane's cousin, Eliza de Feuillide. Her husband, a French Count, was guillotined in Paris.

children from starvation. Rather like India is today. If you were a child and your parents died, you lived on the streets . . . If you stole anything worth more than £5 you could be hanged, or transported to a penal colony for life. If it was under £5 there were long, harsh prison sentences in unspeakable prisons, and the age of criminal liability was seven.

For the most part, only those belonging to the higher classes enjoyed both the skill of reading and the money to buy books or to borrow them from a circulating library. So inevitably, only the better-off would have had the pleasure of reading a novel by Austen. In other words, her reading public came from the higher classes, just as she did. For although Jane often had to worry about money after her father's death, she belonged to the gentry and thus identified with the classes of wealth.

In any case, poverty is relative. It is true that Jane had to save money wherever possible, but she would have considered servants a necessity, not an extravagance.

A labourer's cottage, showing the deprivation and dirt suffered by the poor.

43

A circulating library, which lent books to those who paid a subscription fee.

In other words, she would have felt that she had standards to maintain which most people in England could not even dream of. Her readers would have shared her assumptions about how life should be lived. As a reviewer in an 1816 edition of the Tory *Quarterly Review* observes, 'Emma delineates with great accuracy the habits and manners of a middle class of gentry.' He adds that 'her *dramatis personae* [characters] conduct themselves upon the motives and principles which the readers may recognize as ruling their own and that of most of their acquaintances.' In other words, the author and her readers came from the same class and shared the same set of values.

Today, it is hard to understand the basis of some of Austen's assumptions. When, for example, she asks the reader of *Pride and Prejudice*, 'What praise can be more valuable than the praise of an intelligent servant?', the reader of the late twentieth century – who has never had a servant – is likely to feel baffled. But readers in the early nineteenth century would have been more likely to nod in a knowing sort of way to this question.

Social change

Most people in England were still living on the land when Austen was alive. But within twenty years of her death in 1817, the majority of the population lived in urban centres and were involved in some way in industry. The seeds of this transformation were taking root in Austen's time. Arnold Kettle, a critic who has studied fiction in the light of social and historical developments, explains that:

> . . . by the time of Jane Austen the eighteenth-century world – that apparently secure society ruled by a self-consciously enlightened alliance of landed aristocrat and commercial gentleman – that world is almost gone. The industrial revolution is under way and a new and immensely powerful class – that of the industrial capitalists – is in the ascendancy.

Chawton Manor, the Hampshire seat of the Knights, Edward Austen's adoptive family.

We can see a reflection of this change in *Pride and Prejudice*, which does not portray the static society we might at first expect to find. The nobility, exemplified by Lady Catherine, is shown to be fallible and often mistaken, and there is a symbol of future decline in the physical weakness of her daughter. We see, too, that the Bingleys and Gardiners, whose wealth derives from trade, are gaining in influence.

In comparison with the Victorian era, which was profoundly affected by the process of industrialization, Jane Austen's England seems to have been calm and stable. But in fact, it was creating and adapting to far-reaching change. A historian has observed that since Jane lived 'through the Revolutionary Age, she hoped, as a member of the gentry, of traditional landed society, to see the members of her class adjust to a world that was changing before her, but also she was aware of their shortcomings. Neither attacking nor defending her class, she examined its chances of survival.'

We see this most clearly in *Mansfield Park*, which conveys the fragility of traditional society. The superficiality and self-interest of the Crawfords, as well as the weaknesses of the Bertram family, are a threat to the values that are exemplified in the great house and gardens of Mansfield. Only the genuine and good Fanny has the moral strength to resist such a threat. Her refusal to participate in the 'theatricals' can be a seen as a fight

There was a vast difference between the life of a landowner and that of his labourers.

The indolent Lady Bertram with her pug in Mansfield Park.

Opposite *Fanny 'looked on and listened' to the preparations for the play in* Mansfield Park.

for the survival of the Mansfield values. When she declares, 'No, indeed, I cannot act', she is declaring not only her refusal to join but also the fact of her sincerity. By marrying Edmund she becomes part of the Bertram family and we are given to understand that her influence will save Mansfield and the Bertrams from moral decay.

This apparently happy conclusion, however, depends on the integrity of an outsider, for Fanny is a poor relation, with no natural right to the privileges of Mansfield. As a comment on the future of England, therefore, *Mansfield Park* indicates that Austen did not feel unqualified optimism about the survival of her class.

2 Two Novels: *Pride and Prejudice* and *Northanger Abbey*

First Impressions

When Jane Austen began *Pride and Prejudice* in 1796, she planned to call it *First Impressions*. This title reflects the first – and false – impressions that Darcy and Elizabeth have of each other. The final title, under which the novel appeared when it was published in 1813, indicates the basis of these false impressions. The idea for this title probably came from *Cecilia*, a novel by Fanny Burney, another (and more famous) contemporary of Austen. In its closing pages, a wise character observes that the misfortunes in the novel are 'the result of PRIDE and PREJUDICE'.

Pride

Most of the characters in *Pride and Prejudice* show at least some degree of pride. Collins is a mixture of 'pride and obsequiousness', both Elizabeth and her father are proud of their wit, and Lady Catherine and Miss Bingley display a false pride in their social status.

It is Darcy, however, who is the chief example of this belief in a superiority to others. As soon as the Bennets (and the reader, too) meet him, 'he was discovered to be proud, and to be above his company'. His pride is most clearly revealed in his initial proposal of marriage to Elizabeth, in which 'he was not more eloquent on the subject of tenderness than of pride.' He loves her, he says, but feels obliged to add that a marriage to someone of lower social status (her grandfather was an attorney and her uncle lives by trade) would degrade him. 'His sense of her inferiority – of its being a degradation – of the family obstacles which judgement had always opposed to inclination,' writes Austen, 'were dwelt on with a warmth.'

Prejudice

Like the flaw of pride, prejudice permeates this novel. Even Jane Bennet reveals a bias: she is prejudiced so much in favour of others, that she cannot see their faults.

Darcy annoys Elizabeth at their first meeting by declaring that she 'is tolerable; but not handsome enough to tempt me' (Pride and Prejudice).

Elizabeth in the company of Darcy and Wickham in the MGM film version of Pride and Prejudice.

In Lady Catherine and the Bingley sisters, we see that prejudice is closely related to pride: for their pride could just as well be described as social prejudice.

Elizabeth is so influenced by her 'first impressions' of Wickham and Darcy that she is blind to the truth. Unable to look beyond the surface of Darcy's patronizing diffidence and Wickham's smooth talk, she believes Wickham's stories about Darcy. The interaction of Elizabeth's prejudice and Darcy's pride creates the misunderstanding and complexity that are central to the novel's plot.

The process of self-discovery

The heroine and hero are alerted by each other to the false nature of their attitudes. They can now regard each other with the open mind of self-knowledge. Darcy realizes that Elizabeth's worth as an individual more than compensates for the status and behaviour of her family. He is now ashamed of his former feelings: 'and such I still might have been but for you, dearest, loveliest, Elizabeth! What do I not owe you!'

It seems unlikely that Darcy would have overcome his flaw of pride if Elizabeth had not been so ready to insist on her equality as an individual. Indeed, if Elizabeth had not challenged Lady Catherine's insistence that she should refuse to marry Darcy, he might never have learnt of her feelings for him. Austen evidently admired Elizabeth's strength of character, for she wrote in a letter that 'I must confess that I think her [that is, Elizabeth] as delightful a creature as ever appeared in print'.

Once Elizabeth realizes how mistaken she has been in her assessment of Darcy, she also reaches a better understanding of herself. 'Till this moment,' she realizes, 'I never knew myself.' Austen adds '. . . of neither Darcy nor Wickham could she think without feeling that she had been blind, partial, prejudiced, absurd.'

Elizabeth and Darcy in the grounds of Pemberley (BBC).

Austen's didactic purpose

Austen conceived of her work in didactic terms. She was a 'deliberate and conscious moralist', who hoped that *Pride and Prejudice* would educate her readers in the difference between true and false moral values. The didactic theme is not confined to the central characters, but spreads through the outer layers of the story. The lesson offered by Darcy's mistaken pride, for example, is underlined by an implied comparison between Lady Catherine and the Gardiners. Even though Lady Catherine is of 'noble' birth, she displays 'ill-breeding'. The Gardiners, on the other hand, who belong to the classes of trade, are shown to be capable of real nobility. We are told that, 'The Netherfield ladies would have had difficulty in believing that a man who lived by trade, and within view of his own warehouses, could have been so well-bred and agreeable.'

Marriage

There are several marriages in this novel. The only successful one is that of the Gardiners, which is based on mutual affection and respect. The marriage of Mr and Mrs Bennet reveals little 'conjugal felicity' because 'respect, esteem, and confidence had vanished forever'. Lydia and Wickham are miserable together, because their attraction for each other was solely physical and they have no real understanding of themselves or each other.

Lydia flirting with soldiers in Pride and Prejudice.

"Tenderly flirting

Although Austen stresses the need for genuine affection in marriage, she does not condemn Charlotte's marriage to Collins. Elizabeth eventually realizes that Charlotte's decision is more realistic than foolish, because it ensures financial security and a measure of status. On the other hand, marriage for money alone is not given the author's approval. Wickham, she suggests, is morally wrong when he seeks a relationship with Miss King only because of her 'sudden acquisition of ten thousand pounds'.

The Bennet sisters on an outing in the BBC production of Pride and Prejudice.

Parenthood

The theme of marriage is linked to that of parenthood. There are no really good parents in the novel except for the Gardiners, who offer the Bennet daughters the only real guidance and support that is available to them (we can safely assume that they are good parents to their own children, too). The other parents are all complete failures. Mrs Bennet disregards the happiness of her daughters in her zeal to find husbands for them. Mr Bennet, too, takes little active interest in his daughters' welfare and 'in exposing his wife to the contempt of her own children, was . . . highly reprehensible.' Lydia's

The Gothic castle built at Strawberry Hill by Horace Walpole, who wrote the first Gothic novel.

disappearance with Wickham can be seen as a direct result of her mother's folly and her father's indifference. Lady Catherine is not much use as a parent either, for she shows little genuine interest in her daughter.

This focus on marriage and parenthood, which is linked to an examination of human behaviour and moral values, is part of Austen's overall didactic purpose.

Northanger Abbey

Northanger Abbey was first begun in 1798, under the title *Susan*. It was not published, however, until 1817, five months after Austen's death. A major cause of the delay was the prevarication of a publisher in Bath, who bought the novel in 1803 for ten pounds but then decided not to publish it. With the help of her brother Henry, Austen finally bought back the copyright from the publisher.

Theme and purpose

Northanger Abbey functions as a novel on two related levels. On one level, it is a burlesque of Gothic fiction which mocks the foolish popular novels of the period (though in no way does it mock fiction as a whole). On another level, it is the story of a young girl's entrance into society and her maturation into a sensitive and sensible adult. Each level complements the other and together they achieve Austen's didactic purpose – to educate the reader in the difference between illusion and reality, and between true and false moral values.

Opposite *An illustration from Ann Radcliffe's celebrated Gothic novel,* The Mysteries of Udolpho.

The Gothic novel

The term 'Gothic', as applied to fiction, derives from Horace Walpole's *The Castle of Otranto*, 1764, which had 'A Gothic Story' as a sub-title in its second edition. The word 'Gothic' chiefly refers to its medieval setting, and it is set against the backdrop of a gloomy castle which has dungeons, subterranean passages and sliding panels. Ghosts and supernatural events play an important role in the novel, and Walpole claimed that terror was the 'principal engine' of the work. A mixture of these ingredients came to be seen as the recipe for a 'Gothic' novel.

Walpole chose to write a terror tale because he had wearied of the 'strict adherence to common life' that was found in fiction. Now, he said, he wanted to write something different. So keen was he on the Gothic idea, that he constructed a Gothic castle at Strawberry Hill near Hampton Court, where he could live and dream of those earlier days.

The Castle of Otranto was a resounding success, despite such incredible events as the nosebleed of a statue, a portrait uttering a deep sigh, a sword large enough to be carried by 100 men, and lines like, 'Why do you fix your eye-balls thus?' Numerous terror tales followed, including *Vathek*, written by William Beckford who built the Gothic Fonthill Abbey.

The Mysteries of Udolpho

During the height of the popularity of Gothic fiction (1790–1820), Ann Radcliffe published *The Mysteries of Udolpho* (1794). It is this terror tale that Austen chiefly parodies in *Northanger Abbey*.

In fact, though, *The Mysteries of Udolpho* is different from the mainstream Gothic novel in that its chief concern is didactic: it aims to convey a moral rather than simply to terrify. Radcliffe shows that there is a very simple and natural explanation for events which initially appear to be supernatural in origin. The heroine, Emily, who was born with 'a degree of susceptibility too exquisite to admit of lasting peace', has to learn the difference between illusion and reality. So, too, does the reader, who is likely – because of Radcliffe's clever arrangement of events – to have shared in Emily's mistakes and confusion.

Fiction as burlesque

Usually, a burlesque imitates a serious literary work or literary genre, making this imitation amusing by showing an absurd gap between its style and its subject matter. The burlesque may be written merely for fun, but is often satirical in intention (in other words, it uses ridicule to expose some kind of folly or vice or to attack an individual or group of people). One famous example of burlesque is Henry Fielding's *Shamela* (1741), which exposes the hypocrisy and prurience that Fielding found

The popular eighteenth-century novelist, Henry Fielding (1707–1754), whose books include Shamela, Joseph Andrews *and* Tom Jones.

in Samuel Richardson's bestseller, *Pamela: or Virtue Rewarded* (1740). The nature of burlesque underlines the fact that novelists never write in a vacuum, but respond and react to other fiction as well as to the society in which they live and work.

The Mysteries of Udolpho and Northanger Abbey

Austen was less critical of the Gothic novel than of its reader, who – like Emily, the over-sensitive heroine of *The Mysteries of Udolpho* – seemed to be unable to distinguish illusion from reality. They did not realize, she writes in *Northanger Abbey*, that:

> Charming as were all Mrs Radcliffe's works, and charming even as were the works of all her imitators, it was not in them perhaps that human nature, at least in the midland counties of England, was to be looked for. Of the Alps and Pyrenees, with their pine forests and vices, they might give a faithful delineation; and Italy, Switzerland, and the South of France, might be as fruitful in horrors as they were there represented.

Such readers, advises Austen, should: 'Remember the country and the age in which we live. Remember that we are English, that we are Christians. Consult [their] own understanding, [their] own observation of what is passing around [them].'

For the sake of her burlesque, Austen makes a number of direct references to *The Mysteries of Udolpho*. But it is evident that she had considerable respect for Radcliffe's novel. We can infer this from the fact that not only Catherine, but also the hero, sensible Henry Tilney, enjoy it very much. It is only the worthless Thorpe who declares, 'Udolpho! Oh, Lord! not I; I never read novels; I have something else to do.' In any case, Radcliffe and Austen share a similar didactic intention: to educate the reader in the importance of reason and common sense.

The villain Montoni in Ann Radcliffe's The Mysteries of Udolpho.

We are told from the first that the 'well-read' Catherine Morland cares 'for no furniture of a more modern date than the fifteenth century' and is 'in training for a heroine'. Catherine looks for Gothic excitement around every corner, and especially when she visits Northanger Abbey, the Tilneys' home. Abbeys are common buildings in Gothic fiction, and all sorts of Gothic ideas are suggested to Catherine by the name 'North/anger'. She is so carried away as to conclude that General Tilney is some kind of Montoni, the villain of *The Mysteries of Udolpho*, and has either incarcerated or murdered his wife.

William Beckford's Fonthill Abbey, the kind of Gothic building that Catherine hoped to find at Northanger.

But she eventually learns the difference between the world of fiction and the world of reality. Austen makes

sure that her readers understand the importance of this difference. When, for example, Catherine arrives at Northanger Abbey, Austen establishes a stark contrast between what Catherine expects to find, and what she does find:

> . . . every bend in the road was expected with solemn awe to afford a glimpse of its massy walls of grey stone, rising amidst a grove of ancient oaks, with the last beams of the sun playing in beautiful splendour on its high Gothic windows. But so low did the building stand, that she found herself passing through the great gates of the lodge into the very grounds of Northanger, without having discerned even an antique chimney.

We see, too, that the melodramatic behaviour of Gothic characters is absurd in the real world. When Catherine sees Henry with another woman, 'instead of turning a deathlike paleness, and falling in a fit on Mrs Allen's bosom, [she] sat erect, in the perfect use of her senses, and with cheeks only a little redder than usual'.

Catherine's moral growth

Like the heroine of *The Mysteries of Udolpho*, Catherine learns to rely on her reason rather than her imagination. She learns, too, to discriminate between true and false moral values. The success of her moral education can be contrasted with the failure of Isabella Thorpe to learn from the harm caused by her insincerity and lack of consideration for others.

Austen's observations on people and society

One of the themes of this novel is that terrible things can happen in the real world, without the trappings of Gothic melodrama. Catherine discovers that although Northanger Abbey does not harbour a Montoni-like villain who is guilty of murder, it is the home of a man whose cruelty and self-interest cause serious harm. When General Tilney throws Catherine out of his house, following his discovery that she is not after all the heiress to a fortune, Austen tells us that 'Catherine heard enough to feel, that in suspecting General Tilney of either murdering or shutting up his wife, she had scarcely sinned against his character, or magnified his cruelty.'

T H E

N E C R O M A N C E R:

OR THE

T A L E

OF THE

B L A C K F O R E S T:

FOUNDED ON FACTS:

TRANSLATED FROM THE GERMAN OF

LAWRENCE FLAMMENBERG,

BY PETER TEUTHOLD.

IN TWO VOLUMES.

VOL. I.

L O N D O N:

PRINTED FOR WILLIAM LANE,

AT THE

Minerva-Press

LEADENHALL-STREET.

M DCC XCIV.

The Necromancer (1794) is on the list of Gothic novels recommended by Isabella to Catherine: 'Castle of Wolfenbach, Clermont, Mysterious Warnings, Necromancer of the Black Forest, Midnight Bell, Orphan of the Rhine, and Horrid Mysteries'.

64

Evil, we see, is not limited to Gothic fiction. General Tilney is rich and powerful and has the appearance of a gentleman, but he is capable of serious wrongdoing. Like *Pride and Prejudice, Northanger Abbey* shows that it is individual worth that counts, not class and social position. In a world that permits the devious behaviour of General Tilney, it makes sense that Henry's love for Catherine develops from an admiration for her integrity.

The structure of the two novels

The structure of *Pride and Prejudice* is like that of a web. The threads of the novel are carefully woven together, so that there is no event and no character that is redundant. *Northanger Abbey* is more episodic in structure, going in a straight line from one event to another. Some of the episodes, like the visit to Northanger Abbey, do not mesh very closely with the rest of the book.

Both novels are sprinkled with letters, which reveal the influence on Austen of the epistolary tradition. It has been suggested that *Pride and Prejudice* was first written in the epistolary form, since letters play such an important role in developing this novel's plot. The long letter from Darcy to Elizabeth that follows his unsuccessful proposal of marriage, for example, leads her to identify the prejudice that had influenced her impression of him.

Portrayal of character

Austen uses descriptive detail sparingly. Usually, she tells us very little about the external appearance of her characters. She also offers little authorial analysis of the different personalities. Instead, we are expected to understand the characters from their dialogue (which is a prominent feature of Austen's fiction) and behaviour.

Sometimes, though, a physical description or explanation is necessary. In the case of Charlotte's marriage to Collins, for example, we are given both a description of her plainness and some explanation of her reasons for marrying this ridiculous man. Without such assistance from the author, we might not fully understand Charlotte's dilemma.

An implied comparison between characters enhances our understanding of them. The differences between the five Bennet sisters enable us to understand each one

The five Bennet girls together (MGM version of Pride and Prejudice*).*

Opposite *Henry Tilney and Catherine are united in* Northanger Abbey.

individually. Lydia's foolish and shallow nature highlights Elizabeth's strength of character and developing wisdom – and vice versa. Wickham's deviousness helps us to identify Darcy (despite his errors) as a true hero, because he is seen by comparison to be a fundamentally honest and decent man.

The contrasts between characters also contribute to Austen's moral theme. The contrast between the reserved and well-bred Eleanor Tilney and Isabella Thorpe, who is physically beautiful but frivolous and dishonest, underlines the inner beauty of Eleanor. In *Pride and Prejudice*, the contrast between the snobbish emphasis on intellect shown by Mary and Collins, and the excessively emotional behaviour of Lydia and Mrs Bennet, helps us to understand the importance of a balanced good sense.

Unlike Elizabeth Bennet, and most of Austen's heroines, Catherine Morland is a very ordinary creature

– likeable, but not very interesting! This ordinariness is necessary for the success of the burlesque element in *Northanger Abbey*, for it is set against the heroic behaviour that Catherine dreams of.

Henry Tilney, however, who is witty and well-bred, is rather like a male version of Elizabeth. He appears to be Austen's spokesperson in the novel: we can rely on him to observe and to interpret events accurately (that is, in the way that Austen intends us to!). Usually, this role – that of providing the author's point of view – is located in Austen's heroines. Presumably, the necessary fallibility of the heroine in *Northanger Abbey* obliged Austen to transfer the role to the hero in this novel.

The setting

Austen's economy of description can be seen not only in her portrayal of character, but also in the physical settings of her novels. In *Pride and Prejudice*, we are given little information about the Bennets' home, Netherfield or Rosings. But as with the portrayal of characters, Austen offers information when it may enhance the reader's understanding of a situation. In *Northanger Abbey*, we are given architectural details about the abbey so that we can measure Catherine's vision of a Gothic edifice against the reality of Northanger. In *Pride and Prejudice*, the organization of rooms in the Collins's home offers us an insight into Charlotte's marriage and her practical manner of dealing with it. Austen explains that:

> Elizabeth at first had rather wondered that Charlotte should not prefer the dining-parlour for common use; it was a better sized room, and had a pleasanter aspect; but she soon saw that her friend had an excellent reason for what she did, for Mr Collins would undoubtedly have been much less in his own apartment had they sat in one equally lively; and she gave Charlotte credit for the arrangement.

Intervention by the author

Some novelists write in such a way that we, as readers, are not made conscious of the author's role as creator of the story. Other novelists intervene frequently with comments and opinions of their own; a technique called 'authorial intrusion'. Austen's approach is somewhere in the middle. She maintains a distance from the events

Catherine enjoys the delights of a ball in Northanger Abbey.

in her story but occasionally steps forward in her own voice to address the reader.

There is more authorial intrusion in *Northanger Abbey* than in the other novels by Austen. This sometimes takes the form of an invitation to the reader to share in Catherine's experience. When Catherine wonders whether Henry will ask her to dance, the author remarks that, 'every young lady may feel for my heroine in this critical moment.' Also, sardonic comments on certain aspects of life are sprinkled here and there. The statement that 'A woman especially, if she have the misfortune of knowing anything, should conceal it as well as she can', bears little relation to the story but reveals the author's perspective on the position of women.

Austen's defence of fiction in this novel (which will be discussed further in chapter 3) is a lengthy example of authorial intrusion that has no direct relevance to the novel's plot. It is up to the individual reader to decide whether or not such a degree of authorial intrusion interferes with the novel's success.

Irony

Austen consistently reveals an ironic attitude to life. The most obvious manifestations of this attitude can be found in her use of language (verbal irony) and her presentation of events and character (irony of situation).

Verbal irony is fairly straightforward. In an ironic statement, the actual meaning intended by the speaker differs from that which he or she appears to assert. The very first line of *Pride and Prejudice* is a famous example of irony. Austen writes that 'It is a truth universally acknowledged that a single man in possession of a good fortune must be in want of a wife.' But she does not actually mean what she appears to say here. What she really means, is that 'everybody knows that a single woman wants a rich husband'! This kind of verbal irony pervades her work.

Elizabeth's competence at the piano was one of the accomplishments acquired by young women of her class.

Irony of situation is less easy to identify. It usually involves some kind of incongruity. The fact that Collins is snobbish, pompous and sometimes cruel, for example, can be seen as ironic. For as a clergyman, he ought to be the opposite – humble, sensitive and kind. Such incongruity can also be seen in Miss Bingley's attempt to catch Darcy's attention:

Mr. and Mrs. Bennet surrounded by their daughters in the film of Pride and Prejudice.

> At length, quite exhausted by the attempt to be amused with her own book, which she had only chosen because it was the second volume of his, she gave a great yawn and said, 'How pleasant it is to spend an evening in this way! I declare after all there is no enjoyment like reading! How much sooner one tires of anything than of a book! When I have a house of my own, I shall be miserable if I have not an excellent library'.

Use of language and sentence structure

Austen chose her language and constructed her sentences with extreme care. We can see that each character speaks or writes in a way that is appropriate to his or her personality. Even before we meet Collins in person, we can guess from his letter to Mr Bennet that he is a pompous fool. As the first sentence of the letter reveals,

Catherine is startled by Henry in her search for clues to General Tilney's treatment of his late wife.

his words are unnecessarily complex and are woven together in long and complicated sentences:

'The disagreement subsisting between yourself and my late honoured father always gave me much uneasiness, and since I have had the misfortune to lose him, I have frequently wished to heal the breach; but for some time

I was kept back by my own doubts, fearing lest it might seem disrespectful to his memory for me to be on good terms with any one with whom it had always pleased him to be at variance.'

In *Northanger Abbey*, an appropriate use of language contributes to the success of the burlesque. When, for example, Henry amuses himself by describing the Abbey to Catherine as if it really were a Gothic edifice, he speaks in the dramatic manner that is commonly found in Gothic fiction. 'How fearfully', he declares:

'. . . will you examine the furniture of your apartment! – And what will you discern? – Not tables, toilettes, wardrobes, or drawers, but on one side perhaps the remains of a broken lute, on the other a ponderous chest which no efforts can open, and over the fire-place the portrait of some handsome warrior, whose features will so incomprehensibly strike you, that you will not be able to withdraw your eyes from it. Dorothy meanwhile, no less struck by your appearance, gazes on you in great agitation, and drops a few unintelligible hints. To raise your spirits, moreover, she gives you reason to suppose that the part of the abbey you inhabit is indoubtedly haunted, and informs you that you will not have a single domestic within call. With this parting cordial she curtseys off – you listen to the sound of her receding footsteps as long as the last echo can reach you – and when, with fainting spirits, you attempt to fasten your door, you discover, with increased alarm, that it has no lock.'

The length of Henry's sentences, which consist of a number of phrases linked together with commas or hyphens, creates a sense of breathless urgency. It is easy to believe that when Henry has finally built up to the climax of the last, short phrase, he has captured Catherine's imagination. Many of Henry's words are unnecessarily dramatic and old-fashioned: 'discern' when 'see' would do; 'ponderous' instead of 'heavy' or 'large'; and 'withdraw' instead of the simpler 'take'. No wonder Catherine declares that: 'This is just like a book!'

The effect of such language, especially when contrasted with the usually straightforward speech of the sensible Henry, indicates not only Austen's skill, but also the importance of language to fiction.

3 Jane Austen the Novelist

The development of fiction

Novels seem to have been around for ever. They are easily available, widely read . . . and studied at school. But in Austen's day, this was a comparatively *novel* (in the adjectival sense of being new) sort of book.

Most people agree that the first 'real' novelist was the English writer, Daniel Defoe, whose books include *Robinson Crusoe* (1719) and *Moll Flanders* (1722). He was born in 1660 and died in 1731 – 44 years before Austen was born. In the Preface to *Moll Flanders*, Defoe insists on the didactic nature of this tale of a woman who '. . . was Twelve Year a Whore, five times a Wife (whereof once to her own Brother), Twelve Years a Thief, . . . at last grew Rich, liv'd Honest, and died a Penitent.' The 'serious inferences' in it, he says, 'are fully sufficient to justify any man in recommending it to the world, and much more to justify the publication of it.' Such excessive insistence on the book's worth indicates the widespread suspicion of fiction which Defoe had to defend himself against.

The best known eighteenth-century novelists are Samuel Richardson (1689–1761), Henry Fielding (1707–1754) and Laurence Sterne (1713–1768). Austen was familiar with their writings and her 'knowledge of Richardson's works', claims her nephew, 'was such as no one is likely again to acquire.' It is to Richardson that the credit is given for writing the first English 'novel of character', *Pamela*. In this kind of novel, which Austen

Opposite
Daniel Defoe's
Robinson Crusoe
*(1719), the first novel
ever written.*

THE
HISTORY
OF
MOLL FLANDERS.

LONDON :
Printed and Sold by J. HOLLIS,
Shoemaker-Row, Black-Friars.

chose to write, the greater weight of interest is on the motives for what a character does, and on how she or he will turn out as a person. Before Richardson, novels had been largely 'novels of incident', where the primary interest is on what the chief character will do next and how the story will turn out.

The novel in Jane Austen's time

By the time of Jane Austen, fiction was widely read. It was especially popular with women of the middle and upper classes, who were able to read, had the money to join a circulating library, and had lots of time with little to do.

Since the opinion of women was not taken very seriously at this time (they did not have legal equality with men, and were disbarred from universities and positions of official responsibility), the fact that most readers of fiction were women did not do much for its reputation. Since, also, there were at least as many silly romances and terror tales as there were serious novels, there was a general feeling of contempt for fiction. As a result, the novelist Fanny Burney (a contemporary of Jane's, and

Opposite Defoe *insisted that* Moll Flanders (1722) *was morally instructive.*

The young Fanny Burney, a contemporary of Austen, was ashamed of writing fiction, as novels were viewed with some contempt at the time.

much better known than she was) was ashamed as a child of her 'scribbling':

> So early was I impressed myself with ideas that fastened degradation to this class of composition [that is, the novel], that at the age of adolescence, I struggled against the propensity which, even in childhood, even from the moment I could hold a pen, had impelled me into its toils; and on my fifteenth birthday, I made so resolute a conquest over an inclination at which I blushed, and that I had always kept a secret, that I committed to the flames whatever, up to that moment, I had committed to paper. And so enormous was the pile, that I thought it prudent to consume it in the garden.

Jane Austen felt no such shame about her role as a novelist or, indeed, about her enthusiasm for reading fiction. She acknowledged that some novels were foolish, but held the writing and reading of serious fiction in high esteem. In *Northanger Abbey*, she interrupts the story to offer a clear and passionate defence of the novel and of novel-writing:

> Although our productions have afforded more extensive and unaffected pleasure than those of any other literary corporation in the world, no species of composition has been so much decried. From pride, ignorance or fashion, our foes are almost as many as our readers . . . there seems almost a general wish of decrying the capacity and undervaluing the labour of the novelist, and of slighting the performances which have only genius, wit, and taste to recommend them.

Young ladies, protests Austen with great irony, find themselves in the absurd position of having to affect shame at reading:

> . . . only some work in which the greatest powers of the mind are displayed, in which the most thorough knowledge of human nature, the happiest delineation of its varieties, the liveliest effusions of wit and humour are conveyed to the world in the best chosen language.

In *Pride and Prejudice*, she suggests that those individuals who despise fiction are ridiculous. Such an individual

Opposite *Fanny Price, a keen reader, 'found it impossible not to try for books' at Portsmouth and joined a circulating library (from the BBC production of* Mansfield Park).

The Revd Henry Austen, Jane's favourite brother, helped her negotiate with her publishers.

is Mr Collins. He takes upon himself the task of reading to the Bennet family and 'a book was produced'. But 'on beholding it (for everything announced it to be from a circulating library) he started back, and begging pardon, protested that he never read novels . . . Other books were produced, and after some deliberation he chose Fordyce's *Sermons*'.

Childhood writing

Like Burney, Jane Austen started writing as a child, at the age of ten. But because her family were 'great Novel-readers and not ashamed of being so', she was saved from the sense of shame described by Burney. Indeed,

Jane's family encouraged their budding author. Her father tried to arrange the publication of *First Impressions* (which later became *Pride and Prejudice*), and her brother Henry was frequently involved in negotiations with her publishers.

By the age of 16, Austen had composed a mass of fiction (which is often described as the 'Juvenilia') for the amusement of her family. It is mostly farcical and satirical in nature, revealing an impressive knowledge of eighteenth-century and contemporary works. She also wrote bits of plays, short tales, fictional letters, and many burlesques and parodies of the sillier type of romance, including the epistolary novel *Love and Freindship* (like

A silhouette of Jane's mother, Cassandra Austen. Jane's family were keen novel-readers and encouraged her in her writing.

many 14-year-olds, Jane had not yet perfected the art of spelling!). Her delight in burlesque is visible in the following extract from 'Henry and Eliza':

Eliza then advanced to the carriage and was going to request their Charity, when on fixing her Eyes on the Lady, within it, she exclaimed,
'Lady Harcourt!'
To which the lady replied,
'Eliza!'
'Yes Madam it is the wretched Eliza herself.'
Sir George, who was also in the Carriage, but too much amazed to speek, was proceeding to demand an explanation from Eliza of the Situation she was then in, when Lady Harcourt in transports of Joy, exclaimed,
'Sir George, Sir George, she is not only Eliza our adopted Daughter, but our real Child.'
'Our real Child! What Lady Harcourt, do you mean? You know you never even was with child. Explain yourself, I beseech you.'
'You must remember Sir George, that when you sailed for America, you left me breeding.'
'I do, I do, go on dear Polly.'
'Four months after you were gone, I was delivered of this Girl, but dreading your just resentment at her not proving the Boy you wished, I took her to a Haycock & laid her down. A few weeks afterwards, you returned, & fortunately for me, made no enquiries on the subject. Satisfied within myself of the wellfare of my Child, I soon forgot I had one, insomuch that when, we shortly after found her in the very Haycock, I had placed her, I had no more idea of her being my own, than you had, & nothing I will venture to say would have recalled the circumstance to my remembrance, but my thus accidentally hearing her voice, which now strikes me as being the very counterpart of my own Child's.'

Austen the novelist

All the novels by Austen that appeared in print while she was alive, were published anonymously. The only clue to her identity on the title page of her first publication, *Sense and Sensibility*, was the brief: 'By a Lady'. Subsequent title pages merely referred to the author's previous publications. It was considered that a woman who put her name to her work (unless she were already famous) was too 'forward'.

SENSE

AND

SENSIBILITY:

A NOVEL.

IN THREE VOLUMES.

BY A LADY.

VOL. I.

London:

PRINTED FOR THE AUTHOR,

By C. Roworth, Bell-yard, Temple-bar,

AND PUBLISHED BY T. EGERTON, WHITEHALL.

1811.

Chawton Cottage, where Jane wrote Mansfield Park, Emma *and* Persuasion.

Austen wrote with publication in mind, and she took her work seriously. Nonetheless, she saw her primary role as that of daughter and sister. She was careful not to advertise her writing activities and, so her nephew tells us, kept her work a secret from all but her nearest intimates. While at Chawton Cottage:

> . . . she had no separate study to retire to, and most of the work must have been done in the general sitting-room, subject to all kinds of casual interruptions. She was careful that her occupation should not be suspected by servants, or visitors, or any persons beyond her own family party. She wrote upon small sheets of paper which could easily be put away, or covered with a piece of blotting paper. There was, between the front door and the offices, a swing door which creaked when it was opened; but she objected to having this little inconvenience remedied, because it gave her notice when anyone was coming.

The novels

We are sometimes told that Austen wrote six novels, but actually she wrote seven. The extra book is *Lady Susan*, which was written between the ages of 17 and 18. It is an epistolary novel with a beautiful but wicked adventuress as a heroine. This is Austen's only unlikeable heroine. She is very unpleasant – dishonest, greedy and a cruel mother. Presumably Jane and her family considered the novel unsuitable for publication and preferred to ignore its existence.

As the list of dates at the end of this book indicates, Austen was constantly revising and reshaping her work. Apart from *Lady Susan*, which is not ranked as a major Austen novel, each novel was revised between its original drafting and eventual publication.

It is helpful, however, to think of Austen as having had two creative periods: her early twenties while at Steventon, and her late thirties while at Chawton Cottage. In the first period, she wrote *Pride and Prejudice,*

Willoughby visits the ailing Marianne in Sense and Sensibility, *which was written at Steventon.*

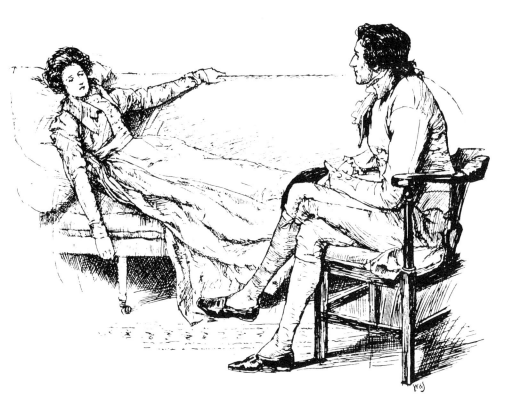

Sense and Sensibility and *Northanger Abbey*. In the second period, she wrote *Mansfield Park, Emma* and *Persuasion*. The only product of the middle years between the Steventon and the Chawton periods is the fragment called *The Watsons*, which Austen started in Bath in 1804. She abandoned this novel in the following year, having completed only a little over 16,000 words. Another unfinished novel is *Sanditon*, which Austen began in January 1817, but was forced by illness to discontinue in March.

All six major novels have the basic ingredients of a classic love story. The heroine and her lover are confronted by obstacles to their union, which is eventually assured. But the marriage is always of secondary importance to the process of self-discovery and moral improvement that is experienced by the heroine (and, sometimes, by some of the other characters). All the novels are didactic in purpose, illustrating the difference between true and false moral values.

Emma and her father in the BBC production of Emma. *There is a depth of emotion in this novel that is absent from Austen's earlier fiction.*

Anne Elliot and her father in Persuasion, *the last novel completed by Austen.*

In some respects, however, the later books differ from the earlier three. For one thing, there is a new and keen awareness of the depth of human thought and emotion, which is especially evident in *Emma*. Some critics claim that this 'psychological' aspect of the last three novels, as well as the manifest development in Austen's narrative skills, make them her best work.

But they are also marked by a more sombre and resigned attitude to life. We no longer find the lively sparkle of *Pride and Prejudice*, with the animated love of Elizabeth and Darcy. Instead, there is a lack of spontaneity, which in *Mansfield Park* casts an air of sterility on the union of Fanny and Edmund. It is as if Jane was so conscious now of the complexity of human life that she was unable to believe in unalloyed joy. Even the apparently happy conclusion to *Persuasion* contains the remark that the heroine:

> . . . was almost bewildered – almost *too* happy in looking back. It was necessary to sit up half the night, and lie awake the remainder, to comprehend with composure her present state, and pay for the overplus of bliss by headache and fatigue.

Fanny and Edmund eventually find harmony in Mansfield Park *(BBC).*

In the closing pages of *Mansfield Park*, Austen declares, 'Let other pens dwell on guilt and misery. I quit such odious subjects as soon as I can . . .' This must be another example of Austen's irony – because the novel is full of guilt and misery!

'A little bit of ivory' . . .

'Though Jane Austen wrote her books in troubled years, which included the French Revolution, her novels are calm pictures of society life.' This twentieth-century comment on Austen reflects and reinforces the common view that Austen's fiction was out of touch with the world in which she lived. It has gained support from her description of her work as 'a little bit of ivory, two inches wide, on which I work with so fine a brush as to produce little effect after much labour.'

But how accurate is this view? It is true, of course, as one critic has observed, that 'Jane Austen's art is very closely bound up with the partial viewpoint of one social group'. This is perhaps inevitable in the work of an author who declared in a letter that '3 or 4 Families in a County Village is the very thing to work on'. Servants and labourers, the providers of comfort and food, are absent from Austen's fiction. Indeed, the country seems to contain nothing but places for walking and the people

Opposite *The kind of outfit worn by women for walking. In Austen's fiction, the country is full of places for walks for its wealthier inhabitants.*

Harriet is 'white and frightened' when she meets a group of gypsies in Emma *(BBC).*

and the houses that are worth 'visits'. When the poor are referred to, they are not important in themselves but merely serve to develop the novel. Emma's visit to a poor cottage in *Emma*, for example, tells us nothing about the distress of the family that lives in it. It is only an opportunity for explaining that 'Emma was very compassionate; and the distresses of the poor were as sure of relief from her personal attention and kindness, her counsel and her patience, as from her purse.'

It is also the case that Austen did not bother to identify or deplore the horrifying inequality between rich and poor. This social injustice was evoked powerfully by her contemporary, the poet William Blake. His concern produced 'Holy Thursday', the poem he wrote in 1794:

> Is this a holy thing to see,
> In a rich and fruitful land,
> Babes reduced to misery,
> Fed with cold and usurous hand?
>
> Is that trembling cry a song?
> Can it be a song of joy?
> And so many children poor?
> It is a land of poverty!

William Blake (1757–1827), whose Songs of Innocence *and* Songs of Experience *evoke the sufferings of the poor.*

But the concern that informs Blake's poetry was not a common feature of the fiction of the time. Indeed, it did not enter English fiction in any noticeable way until the 1840s. So Austen was by no means an unusual novelist in disregarding matters of social injustice.

. . . but a large slice of life

Austen herself drew a clear connection between the world in which she lived and her fiction. This may be inferred from the 'Advertisement by the Authoress' that precedes *Northanger Abbey*. 'The public,' it states, 'are entreated to bear in mind that thirteen years have passed since it was finished, many more since it was begun, and that during that period, places, manners, books, and opinions have undergone considerable changes.'

In many ways, Austen reveals an acute awareness of her social and historical reality. Property, for example, is as important in her fiction as it was to the establishment of social status and power in the real world. Rushworth's decision to 'improve' the Sotherton estate is crucial to the didactic theme of *Mansfield Park*. In a similar manner, Pemberley in *Pride and Prejudice* reveals not only Darcy's good taste but also his concern for substance rather than mere appearance. In front of the house 'a stream of some natural importance was swelled into greater, but without any artificial appearance. Its banks were neither formal nor falsely adorned.'

Power in Austen's time was concentrated in the hands of those who owned the land and property of England.

Questions of money, settlements, inheritances and entails pervade Austen's fiction. Darcy's ten thousand a year and the entail to the Longbourn estate, for example, are just two of the several manifestations of the material world that play a vital role in *Pride and Prejudice*. It is as if, remarks one critic, 'the world revolved around the issues of possession and ownership of land and houses.' But, he adds, 'This world *does* so revolve.'

Emma, her father and Mr. Knightley in the luxury enjoyed by their class.

It is undeniable that the society portrayed in Austen's fiction is small in size. But this smallness does not detract from its depth or importance. 'What is valuable in a work of art,' notes Arnold Kettle, 'is the depth and truth of the experience it communicates, and such qualities cannot be identified with the breadth of the panorama.'

Austen's reputation, then and now

Jane Austen was not a famous novelist in her own lifetime. Unlike the celebrated Fanny Burney and Maria

Chawton Cottage, where Jane Austen kept the company of her family. She never mixed in literary circles.

Edgeworth, she never mixed in literary circles. Not all her novels were published before her death, and those that were, were published anonymously. 'None of her publishers', notes her nephew, 'was generous to her or showed real faith in her.' He adds that 'few of her readers knew even her name, and none knew more of her than her name.' She probably felt closest to fame when the Prince Regent's librarian told her that the Prince, who kept a set of her novels in each of his residences, would appreciate a dedication to him in her next novel (which was *Emma*).

Now, however, Austen is judged to be one of the greatest novelists that ever lived. 'Of all English and American novelists,' asserts one critic, 'Jane Austen is perhaps the most secure in her reputation.' No collection of the 'World's Great Classics' is complete without a contribution from Austen, and her novels are often compulsory reading for students. One such student is Fay Weldon's fictional niece in *Letters to Alice*, who assumes that Jane Austen's fiction must be 'boring, petty and irrelevant' and who cannot imagine 'what purpose there can be in reading her'. 'Aunt' Fay urges her niece to give Austen a chance. 'Do not despair', she entreats. 'Only persist, and thou shalt see, Jane Austen's all in all to thee.'

Opposite *The Prince Regent, who received a dedication from Austen in* Emma.

Glossary

Burlesque An imitation of the manner or content of a literary work or form, which is made amusing by the difference between its style and its subject matter. *Northanger Abbey* is a burlesque of Gothic fiction.

Circulating library A library which lends books to members who have paid a subscription fee. The first circulating library was established in Birmingham in 1757. In Austen's *Mansfield Park*, some of Fanny's money 'found its way to a circulating library' and she becomes 'a renter, a chuser of books'.

Dialogue Conversation between two or more people.

Didactic literature Literature which aims to teach, usually a lesson of a moral or religious nature.

Entail A legal document restricting the descent of an estate to certain heirs.

Epistolary novel A novel written in the form of letters, such as Austen's *Lady Susan*. The popularity of epistolary novels was high in the eighteenth century but waning in Austen's time.

Fiction A written story with characters and events that have been invented. Novels and short stories are works of fiction.

Gentry A class of people living off inherited wealth, whose social status was beneath the nobility but above the middle (professional and merchant) classes.

Gothic novel A novel with a medieval setting (and often castles, dungeons, sliding panels and ghosts) which is intended to provoke terror in the reader. Horace Walpole started this form of fiction with *The Castle of Otranto, A Gothic Story* (1764) and it was popular in Austen's time. *Northanger Abbey* is a burlesque of Gothic fiction.

Hero/heroine The chief character in a story or play, who is usually, but not always, good. Austen's heroines are fundamentally good but capable of error: the heroine of *Emma*, for example, is well-intentioned but has to learn from her mistakes.

Irony There is: a) **verbal irony**, where the intended

meaning of a statement differs from (and is sometimes the opposite of) that which the speaker asserts

b) **irony of situation**, where a set of incongruous events are presented together

c) **dramatic irony**, where the audience or reader understands a second meaning that the character does not her/himself understand.

Narrative The telling of a story. Novels and short stories are narratives.

Narrator The teller of a story.

Nobility Those people belonging to the highest social class, which was also known as the aristocracy.

Novel An invented story of book-length.

Parody An imitation of a literary work, or of an author's style, which is applied to an inappropriate subject. A parody is one form of burlesque.

Plot The series of connected events that holds a story together (in other words, the story-line).

Propriety Correct behaviour.

Prose Language that is written as we speak it, not in lines of verse.

Realist novel A novel where the author presents a fictional world that seems to be just like the real world. Jane Austen wrote realist novels.

Regency The period of 1811 to 1820 in Britain, when the Prince of Wales acted as 'regent' for King George III, who was mentally ill.

Romance A love story. The prose romances of the eighteenth century present an idealized world that allows the reader to escape from, rather than to experience, reality. The novel can be seen as different from the prose romance, in that it depicts the real world.

Romantic era A period of European art, music and literature in the late eighteenth and early nineteenth centuries, showing an emphasis on feeling and content rather than order and form. Romantic writers such as Wordsworth, Coleridge, Byron, Shelley, Keats and Blake concentrated on the divine, the supernatural and the exotic, and advocated free expression of the passions and of individuality.

Satire The use of ridicule and humour to expose and deride someone or something.

Sensibility A readiness to be influenced by feelings and emotions.

List of dates

Year	Austen's life and work	Historical and artistic events
1775	Jane Austen is born on 16 December, at Steventon in Hampshire.	American War of Independence (from Britain) begins.
1782		Fanny Burney: *Cecilia* (Austen took the title of *Pride and Prejudice* from the closing pages of this novel).
1783	Jane and her elder sister Cassandra go away to school.	Treaty of Versailles: Britain recognizes American Independence. Britain concedes legislative independence to Irish Parliament.
1784	Jane and Cassandra are brought home from school with 'putrid fever'.	The first iron-rolling mill is built.
1785	Jane and Cassandra, now recovered, go away to a different school.	The first cotton mill is built in England. Cartwright invents the power loom. Mozart: *The Marriage of Figaro*.
1786	Jane begins to write, short stories, bits of plays, burlesques and silly romances.	First gas lighting.

1787	Jane and Cassandra leave school and settle at home in Steventon.	The Association for the Abolition of Slavery is established. Goethe: *Iphigenie*.
1788		*The Times* is founded. First steamboat.
1789		The fall of the Bastille in Paris, 14 July, marking the start of the French Revolution. William Blake: *Songs of Innocence*.
1790	Jane writes *Love and Freindship*.	Goethe: *Faust*.
1791		Thomas Paine: *Rights of Man*. Boswell: *Life of Johnson*. Mozart dies.
1792		Mary Wollstonecraft: *Vindication of the Rights of Women*.
1793	Jane works on *Lady Susan* which is eventually published in 1871 by her nephew.	King Louis XVI and Marie-Antoinette of France are beheaded. Reign of Terror in France under Robespierre.
1794	The Count de Feuillide, the husband of Jane's cousin Eliza, is guillotined in Paris. Eliza escapes to England, where she lives with the Austen family. She later marries Henry, Jane's brother. *Elinor and Marianne* is started.	Fall of Robespierre. Cotton gin invented. Britain, Holland and Prussia sign the Treaty of the Hague against France. Ann Radcliffe: *The Mysteries of Udolpho*. William Blake *Songs of Experience*.

1795	Jane develops an attachment for Tom Lefroy. *Elinor and Marianne* is published. It is later rewritten as *Sense and Sensibility*.	Haydn: 'London' Symphony.
1796	The attachment between Jane and Lefroy ends, owing to discouragement from the Lefroy and Austen families.	A French plan to invade Ireland is thwarted by a storm. Edward Jenner perfects the smallpox vaccine (which is not made compulsory in England until 1854).
1797	Jane's father tries to get *First Impressions* published – without success. *Sense and Sensibility* is started.	
1798	Samuel Blackall reveals his fondness for Jane but receives no encouragement. *Northanger Abbey* is started (under the title *Susan*).	Nelson defeats Napoleon at the Battle of the Nile (Jane's brother Frank is to serve under Nelson during the blockade of French shipping). Wordsworth and Coleridge: *Lyrical Ballads*. These poems are often seen as the beginning of the 'Romantic' period of literature.
1799		Napoleon becomes First Consul of France.
1801	The Revd Austen retires, taking his wife and two daughters to Bath. Jane is not pleased at the move.	
1802	On a visit to Teignmouth Jane	

meets a man she
likes very much.
Cassandra expects
their friendship to
lead to marriage, but
they soon hear that
the man has died.
In the autumn, Jane
accepts a proposal of
marriage from Harris
Bigg Wither, a young
heir to a fortune;
but she withdraws
her consent next
morning.

1803	*Susan* (later *Northanger Abbey*) is sold for ten pounds to a publisher in Bath, but he decides not to publish it.	
1804	*The Watsons* is started.	Napoleon crowns himself Emperor of France.
1805	Jane's father dies. 'The Watsons' is abandoned, never to be completed.	Nelson is killed at the Battle of Trafalgar, at which the French are defeated.
1806	The Austen women move from Bath into lodgings in Southampton.	First issue of *Quarterly Review.*
1807		Abolition of the slave trade.
1808	Jane declines an offer of marriage from Edward Bridges, a clergyman. (Later in the year, he asks Cassandra to marry him, but she also declines.)	The House of Commons accepts transportation for life, instead of hanging, as a punishment for pickpockets. But there are still 219 offences punishable by death.

1809	The Austen women move to Chawton Cottage in Hampshire, which has been made available to them by Edward Knight, Jane's third brother who was adopted by the rich and childless Knights.	Darwin is born.
1811	*Sense and Sensibility* is published, at Austen's expense. *Mansfield Park* is started.	Thackeray is born. -1820: George, the Prince of Wales, acts as regent for the mentally ill King George III. This is known as the Regency Period.
1812	*Pride and Prejudice* is revised.	Napoleon invades Russia, but is forced to retreat. Grimm: *Fairy Tales*. Charles Dickens is born.
1813	*Pride and Prejudice* is published. *Mansfield Park* is completed.	
1814	*Mansfield Park* is published. *Emma* is started.	Defeat of Napoleon. Louis XVIII is restored to the throne of France.
1815	Jane is invited to dedicate her next novel (*Emma*) to the Prince Regent. *Emma* is completed. *Persuasion* is started. *Susan* is bought back from the Bath publisher. Publication of *Raison*	Napoleon escapes back to France and is defeated by the British and the Prussians at the Battle of Waterloo. Reorganization of Europe by the Congress of Vienna.

et Sensibilité, the first foreign translation of an Austen novel.

1816	Jane's brother Henry, a partner in a firm of bankers, goes bankrupt. He then becomes a clergyman. Jane's health begins to fail. *Emma* is published. *Persuasion* is completed. *Susan* is revised. Publication of *Le Parc de Mansfield* and *La Nouvelle Emma*.	Spa Fields Riots in London over political reform.
1817	May: Jane moves to Winchester for medical care, accompanied by Cassandra. 18 July: Jane Austen dies.	Mary Shelley: *Frankenstein*. Byron: *Manfred*.

Further reading

Jane Austen's major novels
Sense and Sensibility (started as *Elinor and Marianne* in 1794), 1811
Pride and Prejudice (started as *First Impressions* in 1796), 1813
Mansfield Park (started in 1811), 1814
Emma (started in 1814), 1816
Northanger Abbey (started as *Susan* in 1798), 1818
Persuasion (started in 1815), 1818

Minor works/fragments
Lady Susan (started in 1793), 1871
The Watsons (started in 1804), 1871
Sanditon (started in 1817), 1925

All the above are available in Penguin paperbacks, which include a helpful introduction and notes.
Jane Austen's Letters have been collected and edited by R. W. CHAPMAN in two volumes (Oxford University Press, 1932). A paperback selection of these letters is also available (Oxford University Press, 1985).

Biography
AUSTEN-LEIGH, J. E. *A Memoir of Jane Austen* (1870; reprinted in the Penguin edition of *Persuasion*). This memoir was written by a nephew of Jane Austen when he was 71 years old. Although it presents an idealized view of the novelist, it offers some fascinating details about her life.
HALPERIN, J. *The Life of Jane Austen* (Harvester Press, 1984). This paperback biography of Austen is packed with excerpts from her letters, and relates her novels to her life in an informative and enjoyable manner.
HONAN, P. *Jane Austen: Her Life* (Weidenfeld & Nicolson, 1987). Honan presents a convincing argument that Austen was not – as has often been believed – sheltered from the harsh realities of life.
LASKI, M. *Jane Austen* (1969, Thames & Hudson, 1986). This short biography is illustrated and clearly presented.

WELDON, F. *Letters to Alice on First Reading Jane Austen* (1984, Coronet Books, 1985). In these amusing letters, 'Aunt' Fay tells Alice, an eighteen-year-old niece who has green spiky hair and wants to write novels herself, about the life of Jane Austen and about the rewards of reading her fiction.

Discussion of the novels

KETTLE, A. *An Introduction to the English Novel*, Volume 1, part 3 (1951, Hutchinson Educational, 1967). This paperback presents a clear and sensitive discussion of Austen's novels – especially *Emma* – in the context of the time in which they were produced.

KIRKHAM, M. *Jane Austen, Feminism and Fiction* (1983, Harvester, 1986). This paperback study offers a fresh perspective on Austen by suggesting that the representation of women in her novels is strikingly similar to that displayed by the feminists of her day.

TANNER, T. *Jane Austen* (Macmillan, 1986). This paperback offers a stimulating and lively analysis of Jane Austen's approach to her fiction and of the individual novels.

Further information

Visual

Mansfield Park – Improvement, Open University, Guild Sound & Vision, 6, Royce Road, Peterborough, PE1 5YB, (Tel: 0733 315315). This video is part of an Open University course on nineteenth-century literature. By examining the role of landscape gardening in *Mansfield Park*, it shows the many levels of meaning which the word 'improvement' carries throughout the novel. It creates a valuable sense of the world in which Austen lived.

A video of the 1940 film version (MGM) of *Pride and Prejudice* can be bought or borrowed from video shops (but it may have to be ordered).

The BBC television productions of *Pride and Prejudice* (adapted from Austen's novel by Fay Weldon), *Mansfield Park* and *Sense and Sensibility* can be bought for home use from BBC Home Video. They may also be available for rent from video shops. For more information, contact either a) the Video Enquiry Unit, Rm C223, Woodlands, 80 Wood Lane, London W12 0TT, (Tel: 01 576 0202, ext. 2236) or b) BBC Video, P.O. Box 433, Portishead, Bristol, BS20 9SG.

Jane Austen (1775–1817). This video, which is a Nelson Filmscan Production in its 'Famous Authors Series': 'traces the early days of Jane Austen as a girl in the parsonage of Steventon. Bath was the most influential city in her life and a fine series of contemporary prints illustrates social life in the city. The film ends with her great creative period in the Hampshire village of Chawton'. Orders and enquiries should be addressed to: Audio Learning Ltd., 740 Holloway Road, London N19 3JF, (Tel: 01 281 2395).

Audio

Before Jane Austen, Open University. This radio programme, which is part of an Open University course, looks at the main predecessors of the nineteenth-century novel and asks to what extent Jane Austen renewed the novel forms she inherited.

1814, Open University. This radio programme, part of an Open University course on nineteenth-century literature, connects *Mansfield Park* with some of its literary and historical background.

The Development of Jane Austen's Comic Art/Emma: Jane Austen's Mature Comic Art (ELA007) and *Pride and Prejudice – People and Events/Pride and Prejudice – Moral Intelligence* (ELA049), lectures by experts in the study of Austen, are available from: Audio Learning, 740 Holloway Road, London N19 3JF, (Tel: 01 281 2395).

'Cover to cover' readings of *Pride and Prejudice, Emma* and *Persuasion* are available from: Sussex Publications Ltd., Freepost, Devizes, Wiltshire SN10 1BR.

A study tape on *Pride and Prejudice* (1EN5) and *A Lecture on Jane Austen: The Major Novels* by B.C. Southam (NTCF001) are available from Chivers Book Sales Ltd., 93–100 Locksbrook Road, Bath, Avon BA1 3HB, (Tel: 0225 335336).

Index

Picture acknowledgements

The author and publishers would like to thank the following for allowing their illustrations to be reproduced in this book: BBC 16, 32, 34, 48, 53, 55, 67, 78, 86, 88, 90; The British Museum 57, 61; Country Life Magazine 45; Courtauld Institute of Art 44; The English Association 64; Hampshire County Library 27; Helen Lefroy 25; Illustrated London News 43; Jane Austen Memorial Trust 8, 10, 11, 15, 19, 21, 23, 30, 42, 80, 81, 83, 84, 94; Mansell 14, 36, 62; Mary Evans Picture Library 9, 12, 13, 17, 18, 20, 22, 24, 26, 28, 29, 35, 37, 40–41, 47, 49, 51, 54, 56, 59, 60, 69, 70, 72, 75, 76, 77, 85, 87, 89, 91, 92, 93, 95; National Film Archive 52, 66, 71; National Portrait Gallery 7; Wayland 46.